I0475741

1 Introduction

Having undergone dramatic structural changes over the last 40 years, the U.S. renal dialysis industry makes for an interesting setting in which to consider industry evolution due to variation in managerial "technologies" (Bloom and Van Reenen, 2010, Bloom et al., 2012). In particular, it offers an opportunity to consider the role of perhaps the most fundamental managerial technology: the profit motive. This is because, like other areas in health care, the dialysis industry is "mixed" in terms of ownership: some participants operate on a for-profit basis, while others do not. Moreover, the industry has seen enormous changes in structure over time: whereas the majority of treatment facilities initially were atomistic non-profit organizations, for-profit chains now predominate.[1]

Though long aware of the rising importance of for-profit dialysis providers (Farley, 1993), scholars and practitioners have not reached a consensus as to what might underpin it. This is concerning for both theoretical and substantive reasons. Theoretically, it limits understanding of the behavioral implications of the profit motive. Practically, it keeps policymakers from developing an accurate sense of whether or not there are benefits to non-profit ownership large enough to justify their tax subsidies (Schlesinger and Gray, 2006). These benefits are of very substantial magnitude due to the size of the dialysis industry: As a result of the rising prevalence of end-stage renal dialysis (ESRD), around half a million Americans now regularly need dialyzation, and the bulk of this expense is borne by the taxpayer. Indeed, Medicare's expenditures on ESRD alone now account for approximately one percent of the entire Federal budget (Ramanarayanan and Snyder, 2012).

To partially disentangle these issues, I first develop a dynamic equilibrium model tailored to the institutional details of the dialysis industry. The model illustrates how differences in various underlying economic primitives across ownership types should differentially affect the evolution of market structure. I then exploit a comprehensive dataset of over 20 years of linked annual censuses of all facilities providing treatment to ESRD sufferers in the country to see how actual industry evolutionary patterns compare to the model's predictions.

The paper's chief empirical findings are as follows. First, I consistently find evidence of significant

---

[1]Indeed, between 1988 and 2008, the share of facilities operated by for-profit companies increased from 52 percent to 79 percent. In addition, the industry has become quite concentrated with around 60 percent of all facilities associated with the two leading for-profit chains – DaVita and Fresenius (USRDS, 2011). Antitrust authorities have taken considerable interest whenever recent mergers or acquisitions have been proposed. For example, the Federal Trade Commission (FTC) recently required that DaVita sell off 29 dialysis centers in order to preserve competition in 22 different local markets. See http://www.ftc.gov/opa/2011/09/davita.shtm.

behavioral differences across ownership types after controlling for differences in facility and market characteristics. Examinations of the likelihood of exit show that non-profits are more likely to exit on average, and that they are more responsive to changes in the level of demand. By contrast, comparing entry rates across facility types reveals that for-profit facilities are both more likely to enter and more broadly responsive to changes in demand. Meanwhile, I find that the presence of for-profit facilities has a consistently larger impact on exit and output. All of these results are consistent with the patterns that would be expected if for-profit facilities have an advantage in static competition. Moreover, the results – especially those having to do with asymmetric market structure effects and variation in exit behavior – do not support the idea of large differences in entry costs.

These findings contrast with those of Chakravarty et al. (2006), who concluded that the rise of for-profit hospitals during roughly the same period stemmed from their lower costs of entry, and occurred despite having higher marginal costs. My results also run contrary to the findings of Harrison and Laincz (2008) who found low exit rates for non-profits generally, though they did not have data to examine the exit behavior of otherwise similar for-profit organizations.

In addition, I find surprisingly tenuous evidence of the influence of concentration measured at the county level on economic behavior. I show that the average Hirschmann-Herfindahl Index (HHI) for a county has increased by over one percent a year after controlling for market size, but analyses of entry, exit, and treatment production do not suggest that this rapid rise in concentration has produced dramatic changes in behavior. While I find weak evidence suggestive of increased output per facility in more concentrated markets, the analyses of entry rates imply that this facility-level increase in production has not occured as a result of restricted supply of facilities.

Though the evidence that for-profit facilities possess a static advantage is strong, the question of whether the advantage derives from a superior ability to attract patients or lower marginal costs (or both) cannot be conclusively answered. Some of the prior literature (e.g., Held and Pauly (1983)) provides evidence consistent with the idea that for-profit facilities are more efficient at performing hemodialysis treatments. However, looking at the number of hemodialysis treatments performed, I find evidence that for-profits perform more treatments, holding demand and competition constant. While possibly consistent with differences in upward-sloping marginal cost functions, this result could also suggest the presence of demand advantages given that there is very little price competition since Medicare pays for 82 percent of patients. The latter seems especially plausible given that the analyses do not suggest evidence of capacity constraints at non-profit facilities. Moreover, analyses of output and entry suggest asymmetric diversion ratios across ownership types.

On its face, evidence of differentiated demand is surprising. After all, why should patients consistently prefer one type of facility providing ostensibly homogeneous treatments at the same price? Arguably, the evidence can be rationalized by focusing less on patients' tastes than on their referring physicians' preferences. For example, the results for output are consistent with the idea that those physicians that prefer for-profit do so more fervently than those physicians preferring non-profit facilities. Such strong preferences could stem from the growing commonality of formal affiliations between the largest dialysis providers and local physician practices.[2] After all, research has shown that physicians do respond sharply to financial incentives (Helmchen and Lo Sasso, 2010, Hennig-Schmidt et al., 2011, Van Dijk et al., 2012, Swanson, 2012), and one would presume that referrals to facilities within an organization are rewarded relative to those outside the firm. Moreover, this belief is consistent with recent litigation designed to inhibit "self-referrals" by nephrologists vertically affiliated with related services providers.[3] Alternatively, the data might reflect physicians' belief that for-profit facilities consistently provide higher quality. However, this runs contrary to conventional wisdom and much of the existing literature.[4]

Overall, this paper contributes to a number of literatures. First, it extends our understanding of the role managerial differences may play in driving industry evolution by providing a detailed analysis of a specific industry that has undergone sizable changes. This is particularly useful in the health care context given the longstanding argument about the desirability of extending support to non-profits through the tax system (Schlesinger and Gray, 2006). Second, the paper contributes to a burgeoning economic literature that uses the dialysis industry as a laboratory in which to consider issues ranging from quality-differentiated competition (Cutler et al., 2012, Grieco and McDevitt, 2012) to the role of information disclosures in quality determination (Ramanarayanan and Snyder,

---

[2]See, for example Fresenius' page on their relationships with nephrologists: `http://www.fmcna.com/fmcna/PhysicianStrategies/PhysicianServices/medicalstaffdevelopment/index.htm`. In addition, DaVita has announced their intention to form an Accountable Care Organization following their acquisition of the physician group HealthCare Partners (see, e.g., `http://www.fiercehealthcare.com/story/healthcare-partners-davita-merger-turns-aco/2012-05-22`).

[3]For more details, see, `http://www.floridatoday.com/viewart/20130110/HEALTH/130110020/Court-upholds-controversial-dialysis-law`.

[4]See, inter alia, Grieco and McDevitt (2012), Zhang et al. (2011); however, Brooks et al. (2006) find no statistical effect of ownership status on mortality.

2012).[5] While the previous contributions have noted important factors about the dialysis industry, they have relied upon cross-sectional data or panel datasets with a small time series dimension. Thus, they have been informative about relatively contemporaneous states of the industry but unable to explore the longer-run questions considered in this paper.

2 Industry Setting & Data

2.1 End-Stage Renal Disease

A diagnosis of ESRD means that an individual has permanently lost kidney function. It typically arises as a by-product of serious health conditions such as chronic kidney disease, coronary disease, hypertension, diabetes, and other progressive, chronic conditions. ESRD is fatal without treatment, which may take two forms: kidney transplant or chronic dialysis. As noted in Ramanarayanan and Snyder (2012, p. 8), physicians view transplantation as the preferred option insofar as it is associated with lower mortality and healthier lives relative to those on dialysis. Unfortunately, the number of ESRD patients vastly outnumbers the number of kidneys available for transplantation. Consequently, 70 percent of ESRD patients are regularly dialyzed.[6]

Effective in 1973, the Social Security Act extended Medicare benefits to all patients diagnosed as having permanently lost kidney function. ESRD is the only catastrophic illness whose care is financially covered by a national public program regardless of patient age or financial status. For individuals with ESRD who still have insurance through their employer (or union), the group health plan is the primary payer for the first 30 months, while Medicare is the secondary payer. Once the 30 months have elapsed, Medicare is the principal payer.[7] In 2010 (the most recent year for which data are available), Medicare covered 489 thousand ESRD sufferers, while other payers accounted for an additional 105 thousand patients. Similarly, Medicare's expenditures accounted for $33 billion out of a total of $47.5 billion.[8]

Given its dominant role, Medicare has been able to exert a considerable influence on mini-

---

[5]The economics papers themselves complement a large literature in medicine and public health regarding the industry (see, e.g., Lee et al. (2010) and citations therein).

[6]See http://kidney.niddk.nih.gov/kudiseases/pubs/kustats/ for ESRD treatment statistics. See Farley (1993) for more details on the origins and early evolution of the retail dialysis industry.

[7]See, e.g., CMS' brochure on Medicare coverage at http://www.medicare.gov/publications/pubs/pdf/10128.pdf.

[8]Approximately 10 percent of Medicare expenditures actually reflect spending by Medicare Advantage programs. The data can be found in the U.S. Renal Data System "Annual Data Report" at http://www.usrds.org/atlas.aspx.

mum standards of facility staffing and other characteristics relating to quality. It has also dictated terms on pricing. Since 1983, Medicare has reimbursed dialysis centers on a fixed fee basis for each hemodialysis treatment. The payment contains an invariant component known as the "base rate," which covers the bundle of services, tests, and particularly routine drugs for up to three treatments in a week.[9] In addition to the base rate, dialysis centers receive variable compensation for other items and services, particularly injectable drugs (for example, erythropoietin (EPO), iron sucrose, vitamin D), and non-routine laboratory tests that are not included in the base rate. These variable components represent about 40 percent of total Medicare payments per dialysis treatment.[10] Overall, Medicare covers approximately 80 percent of treatment costs; patients cover the remainder out of pocket, or through supplemental insurance policies.[11] Other payers are free to negotiate their own reimbursement rates as for other clinical procedures.

Owing to ESRD's increasing commonality, the number patients receiving treatment has risen substantially over time. For the whole population, the incidence of ESRD – meaning the number of patients newly diagnosed – increased from less than 0.1 percent to 0.35 percent (USRDS, 2011) between 1980 and 2008. For some demographic groups, however, the increase was much steeper. For example, in 1980, around 0.25 percent of Americans over the age of 75 contracted ESRD. By 2008, this figure had increased to around 1.75 percent. As a consequence of both the growing commonality of the condition and its increasing severity (Farley, 1993), Medicare's ESRD expenditures have increased to the point where they acounted for close to one percent of the entire federal budget in 2010 (Ramanarayanan and Snyder, 2012).

2.2 The Retail Dialysis Industry

The decision to have Medicare cover ESRD treatment created an industry of facilities dedicated to providing care to qualifying patients. These facilities are differentiated in multiple respects. The most obvious distinction is between those affiliated with hospitals, which often also provide transplantation services, and freestanding centers that primarily exist to provide dialysis services

---

[9]The level of the base payment has changed several times partly as a result of changes in the cost of inputs but partly also in connection to beliefs about improvements in treatment technology. The base rate is adjusted by a drug add-on payment to account for changes in the drug pricing methodology that occurred in 2005 and by age and body size. One of the changes had to do with the extent to which variation in labor costs were incorporated into the payment. Originally set at 40 percent, it increased to 53.7 percent in 2006 (DeOreo, 2006).

[10]See https://www.cms.gov/Medicare/Medicare-Fee-for-Service-Payment/ESRDpayment/.

[11]For in-clinic dialysis, Medicare covers exactly 80 percent. For additional copay information, see, e.g., http://www.carepathways.com/MedicareCoverage.cfm.

(perhaps accompanied by related testing and/or drug infusion services). After taking account of whether or not a center is affiliated with a hospital or not, the chief way in which clinics differ is whether they are operated by for-profit or not-for-profit entities.[12] Be they non-profit or for-profit, clinics are also differentiated by whether or not they are independently owned or part of chains.

Past research has not reached much of a consensus about behavioral differences attributable to ownership form. For example, the literature has not consistently indicated that for-profit facilities provide better levels of quality. On the contrary, the working hypothesis in the literature has tended to be that the opposite is true, and Garg et al. (1999), Lee et al. (2010), Zhang et al. (2011), and Grieco and McDevitt (2012) have found evidence that for-profit facilities do perform worse on some quality metrics than non-profit facilities. However, other authors have found no statistical difference in quality across facility types (Ford and Kaserman, 2000, Brooks et al., 2006).[13] In contrast to the mixed results for quality, the existing literature is in broader agreement that for-profit dialysis facilities are more cost-efficient (Griffiths et al., 1994, Hirth et al., 1999, Ozgen and Ozcan, 2002). This might help to explain the rise of for-profit facilities, but the extent and implications of any cost differences remain uncertain. Moreover, many of the studies only had access to cross-sectional data, and therefore were unabled to fully account for the possibility of significant unobserved but persistent variation.

2.3   Data

This paper exploits data from two sources. The first is the United States Renal Dialysis System (USRDS), which collects, analyzes, and distributes information about the prevalence and treatment of ESRD in the United States. The USRDS receives its funding from the National Institute of Diabetes and Digestive and Kidney Diseases (NIDDK), a part of the National Institutes of Health (NIH). The data that I use come from the Facility file, which is constructed from the Center of Medicare and Medicaid Services' (CMS) Annual Facility Survey, the Center for Disease Control's (CDC) National Surveillance of Dialysis-Associated Diseases, and the CMS Dialysis Facility Compare database.

---

[12]It should be noted that hospital affiliation encompasses a number of different relationships. The most obvious example is that the hospital contains a nephrology center that regularly performs treatments. It is common, however, for hospitals to affilate with separate physical entities in their service area that focus explicitly on providing chronic dialyzations. The data used in this paper do not permit one to identify the specific relationship with the hospital.

[13]Ford and Kaserman (2000) find that some types of for-profit facilities have identical outcomes to non-profits, but show evidence that other types of for-profit facilities perform worse.

From 1980 through 2008, the USRDS facility data include information on the number of patients treated, facility age (by reference to its certification date), whether affiliated with a hospital, for-profit status (after 1988), and chain affiliation (after 1988).[14] Location is provided at the zipcode level. All other information is at the facility level. Facilities are linked across years by unique identification numbers.

The USRDS data define chains as being affiliations of at least 20 different facilities. Hence, the data provide conservative estimates of the overall presence of multi-unit organizations.[15] Table B-1 in the Appendix indicates for the different chains identified in the data the years in which they were present, their profit status, and the total number of facility-year observations they are linked with. The Table shows that the overwhelming majority of chains identified in the USRDS data are for-profit. Only Dialysis Clinic, Inc. (DCI) – the fifth largest chain by total number of observations – is non-profit.[16]

Beginning in 2002, the USRDS recorded some facilities' ownership status as "Unknown." In order to conserve observations, I assumed that if no change in chain affiliation was recorded, a facility with an "Unknown" for-profit status continued to have its previously recorded status. Similarly, where no change in affiliation was recognized, I assumed that previous years with "Unknown" status have the same value as later years. When these rules did not apply, I left the facility categorized as having "Unknown" profit-status, which causes it to be dropped from the analyses. Finally, I cleaned the data based on the assumption that one-time deviations in status represent error on the part of the survey responder rather than evidence that a facility changed owners twice in three years time. Further details are available upon request.

---

[14]Individual facilities are not named. Instead, their affiliation with a particular brand is recorded if that brand is associated with 20 or more distinct facilities.

[15]In some cases, when a facility changes hands, which has regularly occurred in recent years (Pozniak et al., 2010), the identification number may also change. This may be true even if most staff and location remain unchanged; however, casual observation of the data indicates that there are numerous occurrences when chain affiliation changes and the identification number does not. Nevertheless, this is a concern. However, if there are such errors in variables, it should lead to attenuation, making it more difficult to identify differences. Hence it is a conservative approach.

[16]Examining the connection between profit-status and chain affiliation, it became evident that the raw USRDS data contain errors. In reality, all of the chains are universally either for- or non-profit. However, a non-trivial number of observations assign the "wrong" profit status to a facility affiliated with a given chain. Upon investigation, I came to the conclusion that the problems stemmed from lags in updating a given facility's status following a change in ownership. As a result, I have cleaned the data by imposing that a facility's for-profit status should match its chain affiliation. To the extent that acquisitions presumably took place below the threshold for appearing as a chain in the data or simply among independents, however, the status identifier will contain measurement error. In the econometric analyses, this should make it more difficult to cleanly identify differences across for- and non-profit facilities, and hence is a conservative approach.

The second source of data is the Surveillance, Epidemiology and End Results (SEER) Program, which is also affiliated with the NIH. From SEER, I obtained data on county-level demographic information over the sample period. Since zipcodes do not map perfectly to counties, I assigned each zipcode to the county it was most closely associated with (in terms of population).[17] Since ESRD is more common among older Americans, I proxy for local demand for dialysis services using the county population that is over 60.[18]

2.4 Market Definition

I follow Chakravarty et al. (2006) in considering market dynamics at the county level.[19] This differs slightly from the approach taken by Grieco and McDevitt (2012), and others, of using hospital service areas (HSAs) to define geographic markets. HSA's are slightly larger – on average – than counties, but the main reason that counties are attractive relative to HSAs is that HSAs may span state borders. This is problematic as there is regulatory variation across state lines due to differences in certificate-of-need regulations, which Ford and Kaserman (1993) found to have a substantial influence on dialysis facility entry patterns.[20] Overall, there are 1766 different counties in the data and 32785 different county-year observations. There are 84616 distinct facility-year observations, and 73667 that identify ownership status.

Table 1 provides summary statistics for all facility-level observations. In addition to providing information on facility-level characteristics and the average market composition, the Table provides some sense of the degree of concentration of local markets using county-level HHIs. The HHIs shown in the Table are based on the shares of the number of facilities in a given county associated with each of the major chains identified in the data. Independents are assumed to be atomistic. Insofar as the data only identify chain affiliations if there are at least 20 member facilities, this means that

---

[17]In some cases, the USRDS data did not match prefectly cleanly. Details on how such problems were addressed are available upon request.

[18]For summary statistics on the prevalence of ESRD, the interested reader is referred to the USRDS' "Atlas of Chronic Kidney Disease and End-Stage Renal Disease in the United States," which can be found at: `http://www.usrds.org/2011/slides/indiv/v1index.html`.

[19]To be clear, I am not attempting to construct antitrust markets, e.g., using the Hypothetical Monopolist Test as described in the Horizontal Merger Guidelines. Instead, the goal is to employ a simple methodology that allows me to examine similar sets of dialysis service providers providing similar services within broadly similar geographic regions. In most cases, one would expect antitrust markets to be smaller than the markets analyzed here.

[20]As is well-known (Gaynor et al., 2011), an arbitrary use of geographic boundaries can give misleading inferences when assessing the impact of market structure on competitive tactics. Therefore, all econometric analyses control for market-level heterogeneity that may be correlated with the other explanatory variables. This may not perfectly address problems associated with geographic limitations, but it should substantially attenuate them.

the HHI values are conservative estimates of the degree of concentration. The results are all but identical when the shares are done based on the number of hemodialysis treatments performed in a given year by the different chains in a given county.

Table 2 shows summary statistics after distinguishing by profit status (results for facilities with "unknown" profit status are not shown). Simple comparison of means tests suggest that for- and non-profit facilities operate differently, but also exist in distinctly different market environments. For example, on average, for-profit facilities are located in larger markets and face more competitors. The data also show that the average for-profit facility performs more treatments, while being more likely to enter and less likely to exit than the average non-profit during the sample period. Non-profit facilities tend to be older, much more likely to be affiliated with hospitals, and much less likely to be affiliated with a chain.

Table 1: Descriptive Statistics for All Observations

	Obs	Mean	SD	Min	Max
Pop Over 60 ('000s)	74105	145.9	247.3	0.292	1429
Hospital Affiliated	74109	0.231	0.422	0	1
Chain Affiliation	74109	0.522	0.500	0	1
Time since Certification	69513	9.853	7.786	-1	42
Number of Competitors	74109	12.72	22.80	0	144
Number of For-profit	74109	9.984	20.13	0	133
Number of Non-profit	74109	2.601	3.795	0	20
Number of Unknown	74109	0.138	0.470	0	6
Market HHI	74109	4778	3482	170.4	10000
Treatments	73720	8514	7082	0	245340
Entry	74109	0.0694	0.254	0	1
Exit	74109	0.0177	0.132	0	1

3 Descriptive Analysis

3.1 Changes in industry size and composition over time

Figure 1(a) depicts how the industry has grown and changed in structure over time. Its results are consistent with the massive increase in ESRD incidence described above. In 1980, there were only 1017 facilities. In 2008, there were 5446. Insofar as the Figure indicates that the number of non-profit facilities remained virtually constant over time, this means that the vast majority of growth

Table 2: Descriptive Statistics by Profit Status

	For-profit			Non-profit			
	Obs	Mean	SD	Obs	Mean	SD	T-Stat
Pop Over 60 ('000s)	52628	157.1	269.0	21035	116.6	178.5	23.82
Hospital Affiliated	52628	0.0320	0.176	21039	0.717	0.450	-214.34
Chain Affiliation	52628	0.681	0.466	21039	0.135	0.342	175.44
Time since Certification	49228	8.768	7.316	19935	12.38	8.109	-54.54
Number of Competitors	52628	14.06	24.93	21039	9.162	15.58	32.06
Number of For-profit	52628	11.51	22.07	21039	5.976	13.24	41.73
Number of Non-profit	52628	2.389	3.671	21039	3.103	4.037	-22.24
Number of Unknown	52628	0.158	0.510	21039	0.0830	0.330	23.58
Market HHI	52628	4859	3419	21039	4621	3642	8.15
Treatments	52424	8936	6886	20928	7534	7480	23.44
Entry	52628	0.0790	0.270	21039	0.0397	0.195	21.99
Exit	52628	0.0144	0.119	21039	0.0253	0.157	-9.08

occurred via entry by new for-profit facilities. The increase in the share of facilities operated for profit does not simply reflect differences in the average capacity of for- and non-profit facilities across time. Figure 1(b) shows essentially the same trends for the actual number of hemodialysis treatments performed as for the number of treatment facilities.

Although the number and utilization of facilities grew dramatically, other aspects of the industry stayed fairly constant. In particular, the number of hospital-affiliated facilities varied little during the time that the variable was tracked. This can be seen clearly in Figure 2(a), which also shows that the number of hospital-affiliated facilities operated for-profit remained comparatively small despite the increasing commonality of that type of organizational structure. Overall, Figure 2(b) shows the relative commonality of hospital-affiliated facilities has been declining since the late 1980s. Most of this decline comes from the increasing prevalence of non-profit dialysis facilities that do not have an explicit connection to a hospital. The declining relative importance of hospitals holds if one focuses on the number of treatments rather than the number of clinics, as the resulting graph would look as close to Figure 2(a) as Figure 1(b) does to Figure 1(a).

Figure 3 shows that chain affiliation has become dramatically more common over time. Unsurprisingly, the increase is particularly dramatic for for-profit facilities, though the share of non-profit facilities affiliated with a chain (i.e., DCI) also grew significantly. Much of the increase in the share of for-profit facilities comes as a result of the rapid expansion of DaVita and Fresenius. Between

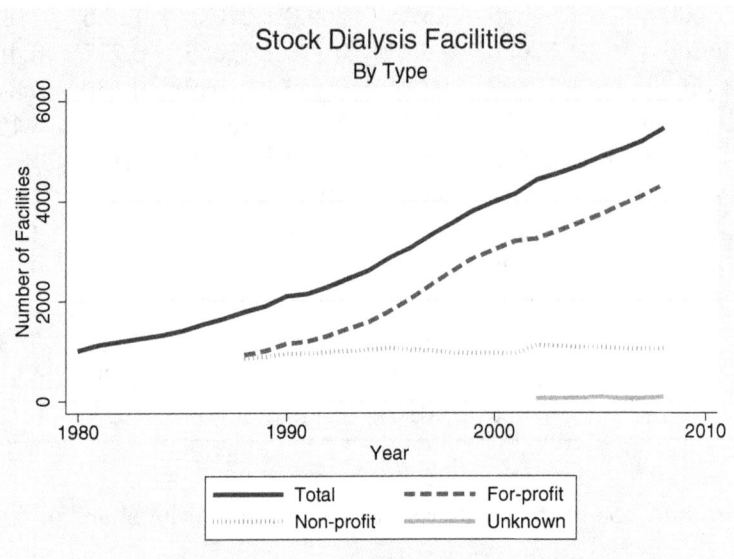

(a) Number of dialysis facilities in the United States

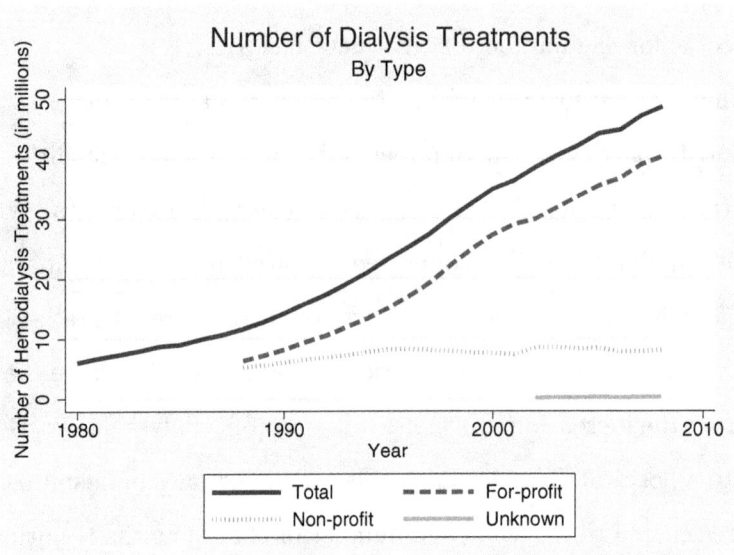

(b) Number of Treatments Performed

Figure 1: Market Structure Statistics

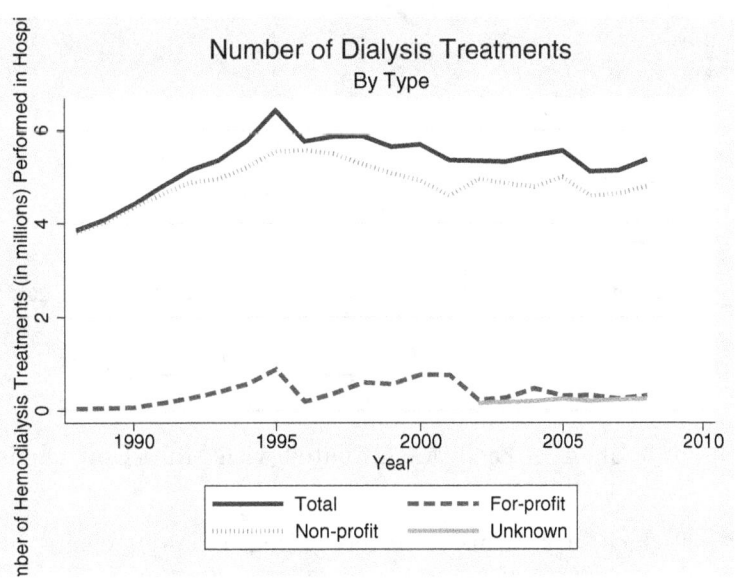

(a) Number of Facilities Affiliated with a Hospital

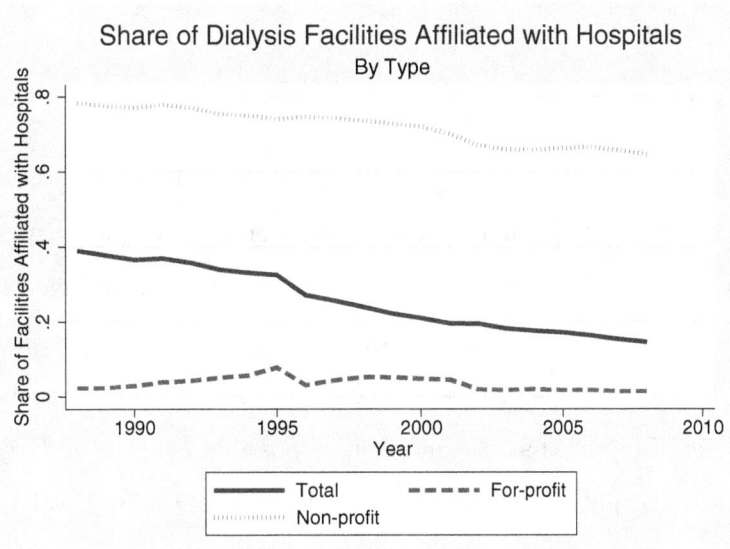

(b) Share of Facilities Affiliated with Hospitals

Figure 2: Market Structure Statistics

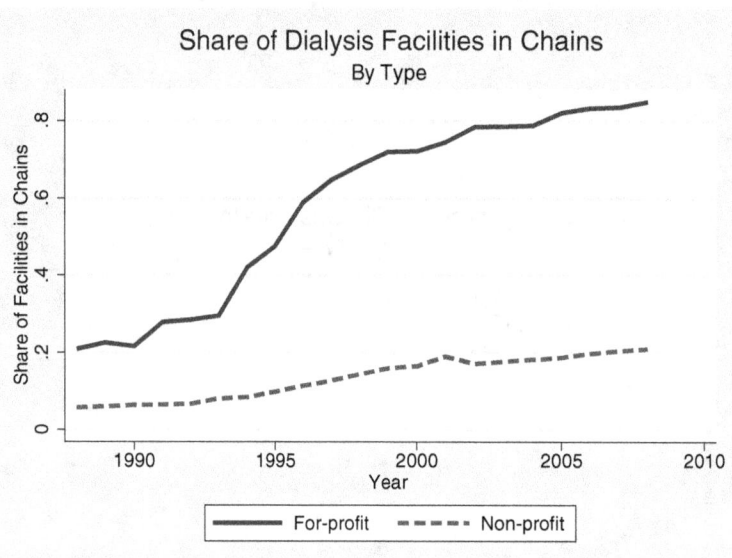

Figure 3: Share of Facilities Affiliated with Multi-Unit Chain

1995 (the first year for which both firms were recognized as major chains in the USRDS data) and 2008, their share of all non-profit facilities rose from 32 to 73 percent while their share of all facilities from 20 to 58 percent.

3.2   Concentration

Figure 3 indicated that an increasingly large share of the overall industry is associated with just a few large chains. However, it did not speak to how concentrated local markets have become. As a first pass at answering these question, I consider the annual average of county-level HHIs over time. Figure 4 shows that by this metric the industry has actually grown less concentrated over time. However, this approach suffers from significant methodological problems. In particular, it does not account for the fact that the number of possible counties is largely fixed while the industry has grown extensively. This could lead to downwardly biased estimates if much of the growth occurred in areas with one pre-existing facility, and the entrant did not share exactly the same chain affiliation. Therefore, I now turn to analytical methods that hold more things constant.

The importance of controlling for growth can be seen in Table 3, which shows the result of simple regressions of the log of county HHIs controlling for the relative size of markets in different ways. In Column 1, this is done especially crudely, restricting the sample to just those markets with more than one dialysis facility. I do this because there can be no possibility of variation in HHI

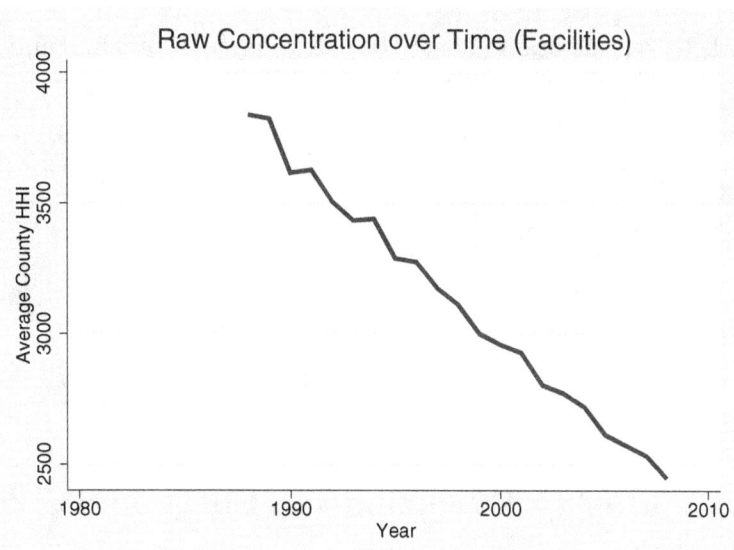

Figure 4: Average Concentration

within markets whose number of participants remains constant at one. The results indicate that, on average, HHIs increased by almost one percent per year during the sample period. This result remains robust when the number of different facilities capable of providing hemodialysis treatment is held constant as shown in Column 2. In this model, identification occurs cross-sectionally and over time across counties that have the same total number of facilities. Thus, the result is saying that as time passes, the likelihood that a county with two treatment facilities would see them both affiliated with the same corporate parent increased. Interestingly, the rate of increase in concentration across different markets systematically varied as indicated in Column 3 which adds a measure of demand (the log of population over 60 in thousands). The results shows that those markets experiencing the largest increases in demand also grew more concentrated more rapidly.

3.3 Discussion

While broadly informative about the changing competitive structure of the dialysis industry, Table 3 – along with the foregoing Figures – leaves unaddressed the key question: What is driving the massive change in industry composition? In order to examine this question while taking account of the possible strategic choice of markets entered by the different types, I now turn to more formal methods of examining industry evolution.

Table 3: Market Concentration (Log(HHI)) as a Function of Time and Market Size

	(1) b/se	(2) b/se	(3) b/se
Year	0.025***	0.025***	0.026***
	0	0	0
Log(Pop over 60)			0.031***
			0.01
Number of Competitors FE	No	Yes	Yes
At Least 2 Facilities	Yes	Yes	Yes
County FE	No	No	No
N	27653	27649	27649

* $p<0.10$, ** $p<0.05$, *** $p<0.01$.

4 A Model of Industry Evolution via Entry and Exit

4.1 Model Description

In order to develop intuition about the different factors that might cause industry structure to evolve, I exploit a model of dynamic competition adapted from that of Pakes et al. (2007) (which is itself a special case of the general Ericson and Pakes (1995) family of dynamic, discrete-time games).[21]

Consistent with the fact that price is largely exogenous for dialysis facilities, the model assumes that competition is between individual facilities of two different types, j, and occurs through entry and exit in discrete time over an infinite time horizon. The two facility types are n and f, which represent non-profit and for-profit facilities, respectively. For the sake of simplicity, I assume that all facilites of the same type are identical. Thus, the model abstracts from variation between facilities aside from their types.[22] All facilities wish to maximize the net present value of their expected stream of profits. Obviously, this runs contrary to the expressed goal of many non-profits. However, as shown in Lakdawalla and Philipson (1998, 2006), the marginal decision-making of non-profits interested in providing output will resemble those of for-profit entities but with lower marginal costs. Therefore, I believe my approach captures the marginal incentives for the industry reasonably well.

The game proceeds as follows. At the start of every period t, each existing facility i receives a stochastic draw ξ_i for the scrap value that the owner would receive if it exited that period. Insofar

---

[21]The specific parameterization of the model used to produce the motivational Figures, as well as details on how it was computationally solved, are presented below in Appendix B.

[22]As discussed in Grieco and McDevitt (2012), this ignores a certain amount of variation in the industry. However, I think that extending the model to allow for capacity issues would not lead to meaningful additional insights, while requiring large amounts of additional complexity.

as there is comparatively little variation in the physical capital at a dialysis clinic (the equipment is largely standard), I assume that all ξ are drawn from the same distribution regardless of type. While incumbent facilities evaluate whether or not to remain in the market, potential entrants consider the desirability of entering. The entrants do not observe the choices of the incumbents before making their own decisions, which are based on whether the expected stream of profits from entering exceeds their stochastic sunk cost draw κ_i^j. Unlike the scrap values ξ, I allow the entry cost draws to be from different firm-type distributions. For the sake of simplicity, I assume that only the first moment varies between the distributions of κ^f and κ^n.

Once the stochastic draws have been received, but before the entry and exit decisions are realized, incumbent facilities engage in static competition in each market m. Demand within a market is given by Q_{mt}. Overall, markets are assumed to be in equilibrium, however, demand is allowed to experience intermittent shocks, which occur prior to the dynamic decisions described above. Consistent with the institutional details of the dialysis industry, I assume that static competition does not involve price-setting. Instead, profits are a deterministic function represented as $\pi_{it}(Q_t, \omega_t, \gamma, c_i^j)$. In the profit function, $\omega_t = (N_j, N_{-j})$ indicates the local market structure (i.e., the number of both types of dialysis facilities currently in the market); γ captures the extent of horizontal differentiation across types, which which would cause the diversion ratio from facilities of the same type to be higher than across types; and c^j represents the marginal cost – assumed to be constant – of type j.

Assuming that the entry and exit draws are independent, and that static competition is done without regard to its impact on future events, these modeling assumptions imply that incumbents evaluate the following Bellman equation:

$$VC_i(Q_t, \omega_t, \xi_{ij}) = \max\{\pi_{it}(Q_t, \omega_t, \gamma, c_j) + \xi_i, \pi_{it}(Q_t, \omega_t, \gamma, c_j) + \delta VC(Q_t, \omega_t)\} \tag{1}$$

to determine their optimal continuation/exit strategies, where $VC(\cdot)$ indicates the continuation value and δ is the discount rate. Similarly, after normalizing the value of their outside option to 0, potential entrants' decisions solve the following Bellman equation:

$$VE_i(Q_t, \omega_t, \kappa_{ij}) = \max\{0, -\kappa_i^j + \delta VC(Q_t, \omega_t)\}, \tag{2}$$

where $VE(\cdot)$ is the value of entry. The solution of these equations constitutes a Markov Perfect

Equilibrium whose existence is guaranteed (though it need not be unique as discussed in Doraszelski and Satterthwaite (2007)).

4.2 Implications for Industry Evolution

Over the long run, differences across facility types in one or more model primitives will lead to different equilibrium market structures. I now turn to the task of assessing just what the comparative statics, as well as the "comparative dynamics," are for various differences in facility-type primitives. These are summarized in Table 4. To support the discussion, I graphical the results for given parameterizations of the model. Details on the model's particulars and computation can be found in the Appendix.

Table 4: Comparative Statics of Theoretical Model

	Variable			
Outcome	Marginal Cost Advantage	Entry Cost Advantage	Horizontal Differentiation	Vertical Differentiation
Entry	+	+	None	+
Entry Sensitivity	+	+	None	+
Competition Effects	Everyone more sensitive to low-cost type, especially high-cost type	None	Everyone more sensitive to presence of own type	Everyone more sensitive to low-cost type, especially high-cost type
Exit	-	None	None	-
Exit Sensitivity	-	None	None	-
Production	-	None	None	+

Differences in Marginal Costs

Economists and public health researchers have long explored the hypothesis that variation in profit status might lead to variation in marginal costs. The general perspective has been that the higher powered incentives provided by the profit motive lead to higher profits (Alchian and Demsetz, 1972, Borjas et al., 1983, Philipson et al., 2010). However, there is also a theoretical literature in health economics suggesting that a focus on output should lead non-profits to behave as though they had lower marginal costs (Lakdawalla and Philipson, 1998, 2006), which has found empirical support in studies focusing on hospitals (Sloan et al., 2001, Chakravarty et al., 2006).

Regardless of which firm-type has a marginal cost advantage, the question of how it would change equilibrium market structure remains. First, it is clear that lower marginal costs should produce higher static profits absent any other differences between the two types. These higher static profits increase VC, which will reduce the likelihood of exit and increase the desirability of entry. Thus, the type of firm with lower marginal costs should be both more likely to enter and less likely to exit, holding all else constant.

Second, variation in marginal costs should impact firms' sensitivities to changes in demand. To understand why this might occur, consider a market in equilibrium where one high-cost and one low-cost firm compete. In this market, the firm with higher marginal costs is the marginal competitor. Since the market is equally split and prices are fixed, its profits are lower, meaning that it would take a smaller exit shock to induce exit. Thus, in the event of a negative demand shock, the marginal firm's probability of exit should be expected to increase more dramatically than that of the lower cost firm.

To demonstrate that this intuitive story holds in the formal model, I compare the computed equilibrium exit behavior for high- and low-cost facilities in the wake of a significant negative demand shock. Figure 5 shows the difference in the change in likelihood of exit following a negative demand shock between high- and low-cost firms. Only those states where it is possible for exit by both types of firms to take place are considered. The differences are weighted by the likelihood that the industry was in a given state, where the weights come from the computed limiting distribution for the Markov process for the earlier demand environment.[23]

Roughly the same logic applies to how variation in marginal costs should influence entry rates following a change in demand. Consider a given market that just supported the existing number of facilities but did not justify new entry. If demand rises, it is much more likely that a low-cost facility will enter than a high-cost facility since they can earn a profit with lower levels of demand than the high-cost facility. Again, this simple story is supported by contrasting the computed equilibrium behavior of high- and low-cost firms following a demand change. Figure 6 shows the difference between the changes in the likelihood of entry between low- and high-cost firms. Once more, I focus only on those states where entry by both types is possible, and weight by the limiting distribution.

---

[23]Out of long-run equilibrium, it is possible for the double difference to have the opposite sign. However, such states would not be expected to occur empirically.

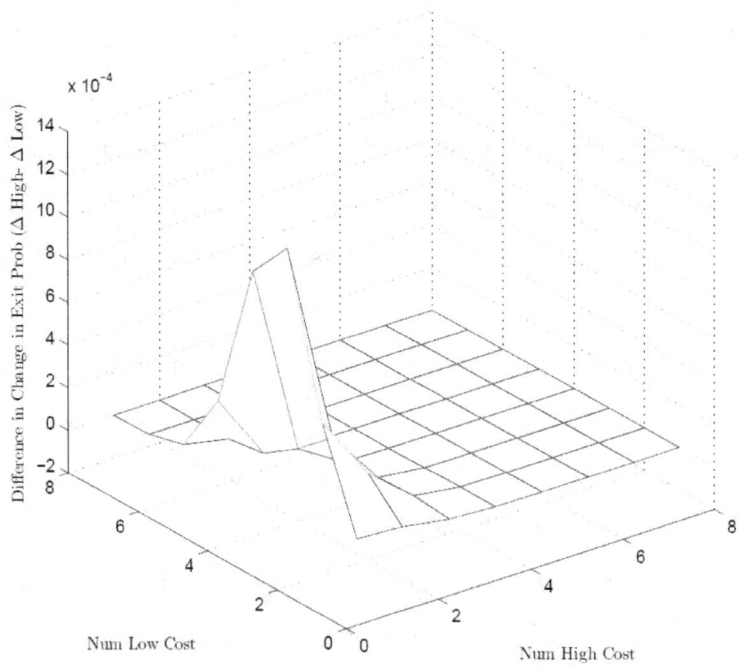

Figure 5: Expected difference in change of likelihood of exit following negative shock.

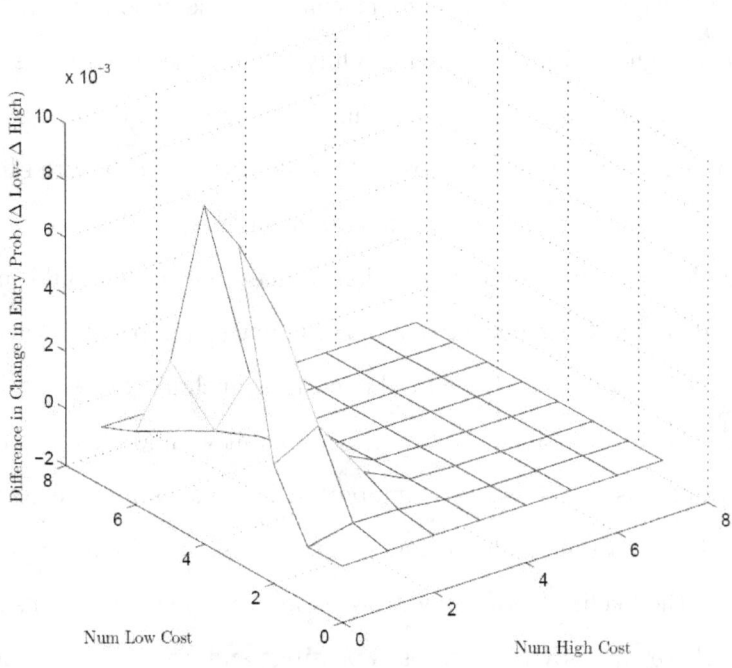

Figure 6: Expected difference in change of likelihood of entry following positive shock.

Third, variation in marginal costs also will lead to asymmetric effects from the presence of different types of competitors. For example, consider an incumbent non-profit facility in a market with one competitor. If for-profit facilities have lower costs, then in the absence of significant horizontal differentiation a non-profit incumbent will be more likely to exit if its competitor is for-profit. This is because the continuing value is affected by the possibility of future periods where the firm has more market power due to the exit of competitors. Thus, if one type of firm has lower marginal costs, then all firm types' expected longevity in the market should be more negatively influenced by the presence of that type since it is less likely to exit. Moreover, unless demand is highly horizontally differentiated, high-cost firms will be more impacted. (The story is exactly analogous with respect to entry.) An example of such differences can be seen by comparing the probability of exit for low- and high-cost firms conditional on market structure as depicted in Figure 7. The graphs indicate, intuitively, that the probability of exit is increasing in the number of either type of competitor, but that the slope for the number of low cost competitors is higher.

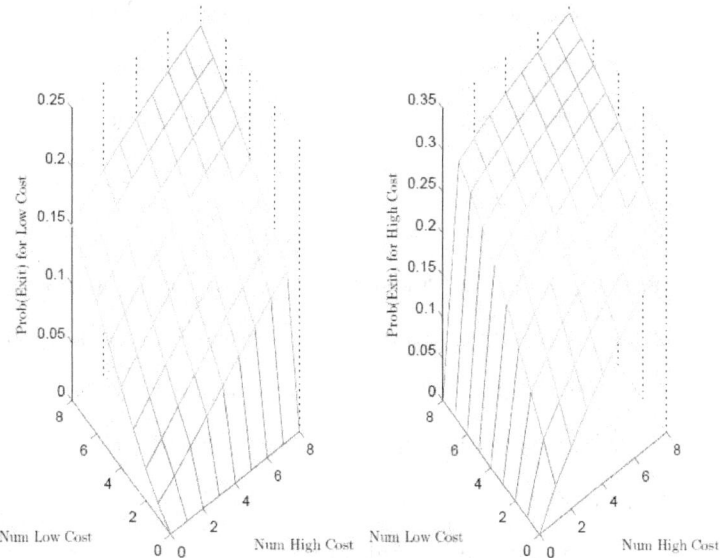

Figure 7: Probability of exit for low- and high-cost facilities conditional on market structure.

Differences in Entry Costs

Over time, differences in the costs of entry for different firm-types could also lead to dramatic shifts in industry market structure. It may be most straightforward to think of entry cost varation as stemming from differential access to capital. For example, Sloan et al. (1990) indicate that the amount of capital hospitals were able to raise from philanthropic organizations plummeted between the 1960s and the 1980s. Chakravarty et al. (2006) note that this was consistent with tax-policy changes during that period that may have negatively impacted the ability of non-profit organizations' ability to raise funds. Although the prior literature focused on hospitals' access to capital, there is no reason that similar arguments could not apply equally to dialysis-centric organizations.

Variation in κ^j would have straightforward effects on equilibrium market structure. First and most obviously, the facility type with the higher κ^j would have a lower entry rate, because they would be less likely to receive draws low enough to justify entering before competitors of the opposite type did so. Thus, we would expect facilities with lower average κ^j to disproportionately account for new entry. Similarly, the model implies that the facility type with lower entry costs should respond more quickly to changes in demand.

Secibd, in contrast to the discussion of differences in factors affecting static competition, it is important to emphasize that differences in entry cost distributions should not lead to differences in exit rate behavior. In other words, holding constant the number of facilities competing in a market, we would not expect differences in average entry costs to cause market structures to vary in their influence on entry or exit behavior. In other words, if the only thing that distinguishes for-profit and non-profit dialysis providers is their costs of capital, then holding constant the level of demand and the number of competitors, local market structure should not have any impact on model fit when looking at the likelihood of exit directly or in response to changes in demand. To illustrate the difference, Figure 8 shows the calculated likelihood of exit when there is no difference in marginal costs, and only their entry cost distribution differs. Consistent with the discussion above, it shows none of the market structure dependence evident in Figure 7.

Third, as for exit, variation in entry costs will not lead to asymmetric competitive effects. This is because conditional on entry having already occurred, the facilities have identical VC.

Horizontal Differentiation

Although the past literature on the dialysis industry has not devoted itself to the possibility, the possibility that facility types might engage in horizontally differentiated competition is interesting to

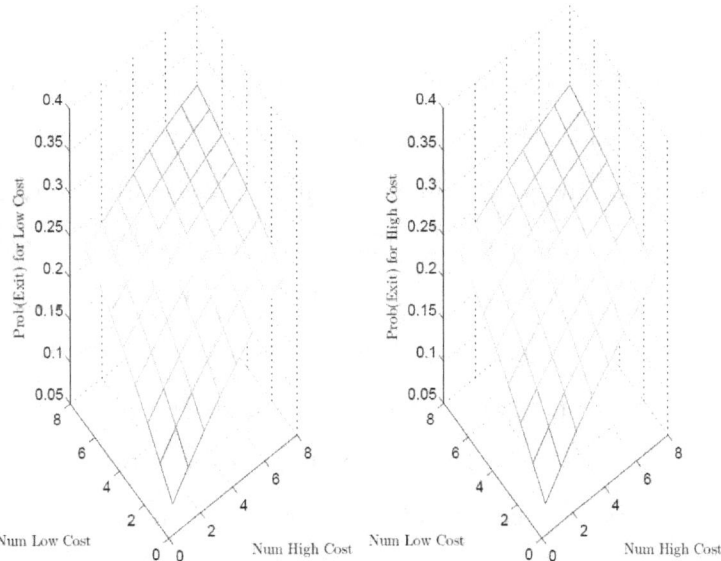

Figure 8: Probability of exit for low- and high-cost facilities conditional on market structure when only entry costs vary.

explore.[24] Such differentiation might occur if referring doctors consistently differed in their attitudes towards for-profit status organizations. The existence of such preferences should be detectable by considering variation in entry and exit behavior of different firm types. First, holding the total number of clinics in the market constant, one would expect higher exit rates for firm i of type j when more of the competing clinics were also of type j. There should be similar results for models looking at the number of treatments performed within a given period. Analogously, one would expect to see higher entry rates for clinics of type j when the number of incumbent clinics of type j was low. These uncontroversial predictions are borne out in the formal model's result (Figures available upon request). Second, while the presence of a low-cost competitor would exert a more negative influence on all types, horizontal differentiation only implies that one is more negatively impacted by the presence of more similar competitors. Moreover, there should not be differential responses to changes in demand, for example.

---

[24]Insofar as price is not endogenously set by competitors, one would not expect to see cases like that considered in Mazzeo (2002) where competitors are vertically differentiated but consumers' willingness to trade off quality for lower prices differs.

Demand Advantage

The formal model abstracts from the possibility of consistent vertical differentiation; however, it is worth considering how it would affect dynamic competition. To the extent that patients or their referring physicians observed any quality difference, it would have the equivalent implications for entry and exit to variation in marginal costs. The high quality type's behavior relative to the low quality type would look identical to a low-cost type relative to a high-cost type. Stronger preferences could, however, be identified in other ways. In particular, so long as the facilities' marginal costs were not upward sloping – a possibility the model ignores – which could cause the higher cost type's marginal cost curve to intersect the fixed price line before the low cost type's, then one could infer from observing higher output that the type of facility was inherently more desirable.

Summary

The foregoing discussion of the comparative statics of a dynamic entry and exit model show how differences across types in the various parameters would influence industry evolution. While there are overlapping implications, there are also many areas of departure. To try to identify which factors appear to be most responsible, I now employ a series of straightforward econometric frameworks to consider differences in exit, static competitive, and entry behavior across different facility types. Their results will be used, in conjunction with Table 4, to try to infer what factors are most responsible for the rise of for-profit dialysis providers.

5   Econometric Methodology & Results

5.1   Hazard of Exit

5.1.1   Empirical Approach

My approach to using exit data to test assumptions about the behavior of for- and non-profit facilities resembles that of Chakravarty et al. (2006). Their realization was that estimating a discrete choice model of exit for different firm types j allows one to contrast the estimated coefficients across types. This, in turn, provides insight into factors such as sensitivity to variation in demand, or market structure, that should be informative as to the relative magnitudes of the underlying paramaters affecting dynamic competition. In other words, Chakravarty et al. (2006) suggest estimating general models of the form:

$$\text{Prob}(D_{ijmt}) = D_j(X_{imt}, f_m + e_{ijmt}), \tag{3}$$

for all facility types j where D_{ijmt} is an indicator that firm i of type j exited market m between time t and time $t+1$. X_{ijmt} is a vector of controls for firm, type, and market variation, and f_m is a market fixed effect.

My estimation approach departs from that of Chakravarty et al. (2006) in several ways. First, rather than estimate separate models for non- and for-profit firms, as Chakravarty et al. (2006) do, I estimate a nested model of the form:

$$\text{Prob}(D_{ijmt}) = D(FP_{it}\alpha + X_{imt}\beta + (FP_{it} * X_{imt})\delta + f_i + e_{imt}), \tag{4}$$

where FP_{it} is an indicator variable that takes a value of 1 if i is a for-profit facility. This nested approach allows more direct testing of the hypothesis that different explanatory variables have an equivalent impact on both types of facility. In essence, one simply examines the δ coefficients, which will indicate the degree to which for-profit facilities differ in their behavior from otherwise identical non-profit ones. Since both FP and the X are separately controlled for, this represents a differences-in-differences approach to identification.

In X, I proxy for the level of demand using the log of the population over 60 (in 1000s) in the county. Following Berry (1992), I approximate the market structure ω_{mt} as $\ln(N_{mt} + 1)$, i.e., the log of the number of competing facilities in the market. In some models, I disaggregate this variable to allow for different effects from different types of facilities. In such cases, I allow $\omega_{mt} = [\ln(N_{1t} + 1), ..., \ln(N_{jt} + 1), ..., \ln(N_{Jt+1})]$. To address the possibility that there are important time-varying, facility-level factors that might be associated with both exit and organizational status, I include indicator variables for whether or not the facility is connected to a hospital. I also include information on the time since its certification date. Otherwise one might worry about confounding the effect of age with that of non-profit status given that type of facility's early prevalence. To explore the possibility that chain affiliation makes a difference, I examine whether including controls for membership in large chains makes a difference. Finally, in some models, I also include information on the degree of concentration in the market.[25]

All models also include year-effects interacted with facility type. These controls should address the possibility that different types of firms react differently to regulatory changes affecting all firms simultaneously.[26]

My second major difference from the approach taken in Chakravarty et al. (2006) is that my preferred models include firm-specific effects, f_i. The inclusion of these controls help to address the possibility of substantial omitted variable bias due to time-invariant characteristics of individual facilities. In other words, they account for the possibility that facilities may possess unobservables that lead to an increased likelihood of exit (or lack of exit). In the current context, the most obvious candidates for such unobserved factors are location characteristics or managerial differences. Because these factors seem plausibly correlated with the included controls, my preferred, conservative approach is to estimate the model with fixed effects (FE). In their absence, one might reasonably fear that the estimated effects only reflected the correlation between the dependent and independent variables as a result of their mutual correlation with the omitted factors.[27]

The advantages of the fixed effect models come at the cost of identifying effects off of the subset of facilities that ultimately exit but which do not exit in their first (only) period in the sample. For this reason, the length of my sample is especially beneficial as it includes 1198 different exiting facilities out of a total of 6654 facilities included in the FE models. Thus, one does not need to worry greatly that results are being driven by an unusual subset. It should be noted, however, that the amount of within-facility variation in factors like hospital and chain affiliation tends to be quite small. Thus, care must be taken in assessing the results for those variables given the inclusion of facility-level fixed effects.

My preferred approach to estimation is to use linear probability models (LPMs), accounting for concerns about heteroskedasticity by clustering at the facility-level. Though there are legitimate theoretical concerns about LPMs, Wooldridge (2002, p. 454-5) notes that in practice their estimates

---

[25]It should be recognized that this follows most of the literature in taking what Gaynor and Town (2011) describe as the "Structure-Conduct-Performance" approach to modeling the influence of concentration and competition. It is admittedly atheoretical insofar as there is no theoretical model that directly links HHIs to industry behavior. However, I believe – in line with the large literature following the approach – that this approach should be broadly informative about the impact of concentration if concentration has a major impact.

[26]Robustness checks that included state-level time-trends for both for-profit and non-profits did not lead to qualitatively different results and are not included in the paper. Details are available upon request.

[27]See, for example, Allison and Christakis (2006) for a lucid discussion of the importance of accounting for unit level heterogeneity in another hazard model setting.

tend to do a good job of approximating the marginal effects of common covariates. Consistent with this, models estimated using Chamberlain's fixed effect logit model in Table B-2 in the Appendix lead to qualitatively similar results.[28] Moreover, if one calculates the approximate marginal effects for the logit models using the standard approach of multiplying the estimated coefficient by the average probability of exit times one minus the average probability of exit, the results are larger but of similar magnitudes to those from the linear models. Hence, I believe that estimation via OLS leads to reasonable estimates of the relationships of interest.

5.1.2 Results

Table 5 contains the results of six different approaches to estimating Equation (5). They differ in how they model the competitive environment and account for facility-level heterogeneity. Columns 1 and 2 omit facility FE. They differ in that only Column 2 includes controls for chain affiliation. Columns 3 and 4 are exactly analogous, but now include the controls for time-invariant station-level heterogeneity. Column 5 retains the chain controls and allows for the possibility of different competitive impacts from the different types of facilities, while Column 6 adds the log of HHI to control for local market concentration.

The dramatic differences in the estimated coefficients between the models with and without facility-level FE suggests the importance of accounting for systematic unobserved differences across them. The differences strongly suggest that the potentially more efficient OLS models are biased. In line with this, several of the results in the non-FE models do not seem reasonable. In particular, they suggest that the survival of non-profit facilities is unaffected by the level of local demand, a result that seems implausible on its face. For these reasons, I much prefer the facility FE models and only discuss them going forward.

Between the facility fixed effects and year-facility-type indicator variables, a for-profit indicator variable cannot be identified in the FE models. Therefore, at the base of each column, I report the average predicted unobserved but time-invariant impact on the likelihood of exit for for-profit and non-profit facilities (i.e., $\bar{\bar{f}}_i$). I do this only for those facilities in markets where both types of facilities are present to preclude the possibility of large market selection effects. The $\bar{\bar{f}}_i$ values should be reflective of consistent unobserved, type-specific variation in behavior and should be

---

[28]The only significant exception is for concentration, which may have to do with the inability to control for time effects in the discrete choice models; including even a year trend causes the models not to converge.

27

Table 5: Likelihood of Exit as a Function of Demand & Competition

	(1) b/se	(2) b/se	(3) b/se	(4) b/se	(5) b/se	(6) b/se
Log(Pop over 60)	0.013	0.014	-0.066***	-0.067***	-0.045***	-0.051***
	0.02	0.02	0.01	0.01	0.01	0.01
Log(Pop over 60) * For-Profit	-0.074***	-0.073***	0.026***	0.026***	0.011*	0.016***
	0.02	0.02	0.01	0.01	0.01	0.01
Hospital Affiliated	0.015***	0.010**	-0.105***	-0.105***	-0.108***	-0.110***
	0	0.01	0.02	0.02	0.02	0.02
Hospital Affiliated * For-profit	0.018**	0.020**	0.039***	0.041***	0.042***	0.042***
	0.01	0.01	0.01	0.01	0.01	0.01
Time since certification	0.001***	0.001***	0	0	0	0
	0	0	0	0	0	0
Time since certification * For-profit	0	0	0.001**	0.001**	0.001**	0.001**
	0	0	0	0	0	0
Log(Number of Competitors)	0.093***	0.093***	0.077***	0.077***		
	0.01	0.01	0.01	0.01		
Log(Number of Competitors) * For-profit	-0.035***	-0.035***	-0.042***	-0.042***		
	0.01	0.01	0.01	0.01		
Log(Number of For-profit)					0.037***	0.030***
					0	0
Log(Number of For-profit) * For-profit					-0.013**	-0.008
					0.01	0
Log(Number of Non-profit)					0.023***	0.002
					0.01	0.01
Log(Number of Non-profit * For-profit)					-0.022***	-0.005
					0.01	0.01
Log(Number of Unknown)					-0.014*	-0.005
					0.01	0.01
Log(Number of Unknown) * For-profit					0.009	0.001
					0.01	0.01
Log(HHI)						-0.034***
						0.01
Log(HHI) * For-profit						0.028***
						0.01
P(Exit) for Non-profit			0.05	0.06	0.06	0.06
P(Exit) for For-profit			-0.01	-0.02	-0.01	-0.01
P-value of H0: diff == 0			0.00	0.00	0.00	0.00
Status * Year FE	Yes	Yes	Yes	Yes	Yes	Yes
Facility FE	No	No	Yes	Yes	Yes	Yes
Chain FE	No	Yes	No	Yes	Yes	Yes
Status * County FE	Yes	Yes	No	No	No	No
Observations	69159	69159	69159	69159	69159	69159

* $p<0.10$, ** $p<0.05$, *** $p<0.01$ in 2-sided tests. + $p< 0.1$ in 1-sided test. All standard errors clustered at the facility level.

informative as to the underlying likelihood of exit for the different types. To help assess whether any differences are of statistical significance, I report the p-value for the t-statistic assessing whether the two averages are statistically different from each other.[29]

Overall, the results provide strong evidence that for- and non-profit dialysis clinics operate in quite dissimilar fashions. This is in line with the simple graphs presented above, which showed very divergent trends for the two types of dialysis providers. In particular, the average unobserved factors of for-profit facilities make them much less likely to exit in all models. As noted above, this may suggest that for-profits have have an advantage in static competition. Moreover, it runs contrary to what would be expected if there were only differences in entry costs. Although the magnitude of the difference between $\bar{\hat{f}}_i$ may appear small, it should be viewed in the context of the unconditional likelihood of exit, which is under 2 percent. Thus, the 6 percentage point difference between for-profit and non-profit facilities is of very large economic significance.

In addition, each model suggests that for-profit facilities' likelihood of exit is statistically significantly less sensitive to changes in the level of demand. As discussed above, greater sensitivity is consistent with being the marginal competitor. Thus, the models' results again suggest a static disadvantage for non-profit dialysis facilities. Once more, as the difference is of economic as well as statistical significance. Using the estimated coefficients in Column 4, a one standard deviation decrease in population over 60 (i.e., 247,300) increases the likelihood of non-profit exit by 28 percent; by contrast, it would only increase the likelihood of for-profit exit by 19 percent.

In addition, the results in Table 5 indicate asymmetric effects from the presence of different types of competitors. Although both facility types' likelihood of exit is increasing especially rapidly in the number of for-profit competitors, non-profit competitors are much more impacted by the presence of other non-profit facilites than are their for-profit competitors. Indeed, Columns 3 and 4 suggest that the number of non-profits has no competitive impact at all upon for-profit clinics. As indicated in Table 4, such asymmetric effects could, but need not, indicate horizontally differentiated demand as well as the fact that for-profit facilities possess advantages in static competition.

Asymmetric competition effects from the presence of different types of facilities is difficult to reconcile with many alternative stories about industry behavior. In particular, it is hard to

---

[29]In other words, I am comparing the averages of the estimated $\hat{f}_i$. One might also focus on the predicted likelihoods of exit after netting out the facility-specific factors like affiliation with a hospital or age. Preliminary work along these lines does not point to large qualitative differences.

understand why – all else constant – a non-profit should care about the character of its competition if its mission is simply to provide services to populations that would otherwise go untreated. Therefore, I do not think that differences in behavior can be attributed to the ostensible differences in objective function between for-profit and non-profit facilities.

Across the different models, I find broadly intuitive estimated impacts for the facility-level control factors. Facilities connected to hospitals are less likely to exit, which is consistent with the idea that they are larger investments, capable of performing more services. Thus, on average, it would take a much larger draw from the scrap value distribution in order to induce them to exit. By contrast, time since certification is weakly associated with exit. Interestingly, both factors are more associated with the exit of for-profit facilities. The results of the sixth model imply that more concentrated markets experience less exit, though the effects are larger for non-profit than for-profit facilities.

Ultimately, the results are consistent with all elements of the hypothesis that for-profit facilities have lower marginal costs. Similarly, they could be in line with the the presence of some degree of differentiated demand. However, their implications run strongly against the possibility that the driver of for-profit facilities' rise in prominence can be attributed to lower entry costs or other factors.

5.2 Utilization

5.2.1 Empirical Approach

In order to further assess the competitive relationship between for- and non-profit dialysis treatment centers, I exploit the USRDS data's inclusion of utilization statistics. The overall goal, much as for the exit analyses, is to see how the number of hemodialysis treatments that a facility performs in a year changes depending on its profit status as well as market characteristics. Thus, I again estimate models of the form:

$$H_{ijmt} = H(FP_{it}\alpha + X_{imt}\beta + (FP_{it} * X_{ijmt})\delta + f_i + e_{ijmt}), \tag{5}$$

where H_{ijmt} is the log of the number of hemodialysis treatments performed by the facility in a given period. Although I continue to allow for the possibility of different demand effects across facility-types, theory offers little guidance as to its impact on output. Once more, I estimate the model with facility fixed effects using OLS while allowing for the possibility that the standard errors are clustered at the facility level.

5.2.2 Results

Table 6 reports the results of four models of hemodialysis treatments. The specifications are exactly analogous to the last four shown in Table 5. The first model omits chain fixed effects and does not distinguish between the competitive influence of different types of facilities. The second model adds chain fixed effects, while the third allows for differences in the impacts of for- and non-profit facilities. The fourth model adds controls for the levels of concentration in the market. As before, at the base of each column, I report the average predicted unobserved but time-invariant effects on output for for-profit and non-profit facilities, limiting attention to those facilities in markets where both types of facilities are present.

Examining the average unobserved production effect suggests that for-profit facilities are innately more productive at any level of demand. Indeed, in the considered markets, the results suggest an average 15 percentage point difference in output between for- and non-profit facilities. This could be consistent with the hypothesis that for-profit facilities have a static advantage in either providing care or attracting patients. For example, if – contrary to the theoretic model's assumption of constant marginal costs – facilities' marginal cost functions slope upward, then the facility type with higher marginal costs might perform fewer treatments if their marginal cost curve intersected the fixed price line before the point implied by their share of residual demand under the assumption of constant marginal costs. An extreme example of this would be if non-profits are more capacity constrained. Alternatively, they could be providing more care because ceteris paribus their residual demand curves are higher as a result of some degree of vertical differentiation.

The results suggest that firm-type has no consistent impact on how the number of treatments performed by a given facility change in response to a percentage change in demand. This is somewhat misleading insofar as the log-log specification implies that as demand grows the proportion of treatments performed by facilities would stay the same. Thus, the difference in the proportion of patients treated by competing for- and non-profit would not converge. The estimated coefficient of 0.67 from Column 3 implies that in response to a 10 percent increase in the demand proxy, the number of treatments performed by each facility would rise, on average, by 6.7 percent. This is quite a strong supply response, suggesting that facilities are not very capacity-constrained or can comparatively easily increase capacity in response to demand changes. The latter story seems particularly likely insofar as facilities are usually small enough to fit in strip-malls and require little in the way of heavy capital equipment. While the skilled labor that is required may not be universally abundant, the ratio of necessary personnel to patients is not likely to be high.

Given that non-profits appear to be able to ramp up production in the wake of demand increases, this suggests that a key part of the reason that for-profits perform more dialysis treatments is that they possess an advantage in attracting patients. Such a finding is consistent with the vertical move of several of the major dialysis chains into affiliations and partnerships with local providers.[30] Insofar as their compensation would be expected to correlate strongly with patients referred intra-organization, one would expect such doctors to have strong attachments to facilities related to their employer (Helmchen and Lo Sasso, 2010, Hennig-Schmidt et al., 2011, Van Dijk et al., 2012), which might produce the observed correlations in the data. Anecdotally, the existence of a Florida law that explicitly constrains Florida's nephrologists from referring their patients to affiliated institutions suggests that it occurs in practice as well.[31]

The results for utilization also lend some support to the idea that demand is horizontally differentiated. For example, in Columns 3 and 4 show that production at both types is disproportionately negatively impacted by the presence of similar competitors. Whereas non-profits are roughly equivalently impacted by the presence of either type of competitor, for-profits are much more affected by the presence of for-profit competitors. This may suggest that some doctors weakly prefer to direct patients to non-profit facilites, while others are much more likely to refer patients to for-profit facilities.

The remaining results are broadly consistent with intuition. Hospital affiliation is associated with a 15-20 percent decrease in hemodialysis treatments for non-profit facilities, and a 40-50 percent decrease for for-profits. The direction of these effects accords with the idea that hospital-affiliated dialysis facilities may have the capability to provide more specialized care, the returns (financial and otherwise) of which may be much higher to operator and patients alike. Thus, one would expect

---

[30]See, e.g., http://www.ama-assn.org/amednews/2012/06/04/bisf0607.htm.

[31]As previously noted, see http://www.floridatoday.com/viewart/20130110/HEALTH/130110020/Court-upholds-controversial-dialysis-law for more details.

Table 6: (Log) Number of Hemodialysis Treatments as a Function of Demand & Competition

	(1) b/se	(2) b/se	(3) b/se	(4) b/se
Log(Pop over 60)	0.780***	0.767***	0.667***	0.674***
	0.07	0.07	0.07	0.07
Log(Pop over 60) * For-Profit	-0.023	-0.02	-0.012	-0.014
	0.04	0.04	0.04	0.04
Hospital Affiliated	-0.184**	-0.191**	-0.160*	-0.156*
	0.09	0.09	0.09	0.09
Hospital Affiliated * For-profit	-0.301***	-0.254***	-0.270***	-0.270***
	0.07	0.07	0.07	0.07
Time since certification	0.014**	0.015**	0.013**	0.013**
	0.01	0.01	0.01	0.01
Time since certification * For-profit	-0.009**	-0.012***	-0.011**	-0.011**
	0	0	0	0
Log(Number of Competitors)	-0.588***	-0.583***		
	0.04	0.04		
Log(Number of Competitors) * For-profit	0.079*	0.080*		
	0.04	0.04		
Log(Number of For-profit)			-0.349***	-0.343***
			0.03	0.03
Log(Number of For-profit) * For-profit			0.004	0.002
			0.03	0.04
Log(Number of Non-profit)			-0.299***	-0.283***
			0.05	0.05
Log(Number of Non-profit) * For-profit			0.109**	0.101**
			0.05	0.05
Log(Number of Unknown)			-0.063	-0.07
			0.06	0.06
Log(Number of Unknown) * For-profit			0.024	0.028
			0.07	0.06
Log(HHI)				0.026
				0.04
Log(HHI) * For-profit				-0.01
				0.04
Prediction for Non-profit	-0.21	-0.21	-0.21	-0.21
Prediction for For-profit	-0.09	-0.08	-0.06	-0.06
P-value of H0: diff == 0	0.00	0.00	0.00	0.00
Status * Year FE	Yes	Yes	Yes	Yes
Facility FE	Yes	Yes	Yes	Yes
Chain FE	No	Yes	Yes	Yes
N	65373	65373	65373	65373

* $p<0.10$, ** $p<0.05$, *** $p<0.01$ in 2-sided tests. + $p< 0.1$ in 1-sided test. All standard errors clustered at the facility level.

them to perform fewer dialyzations all else equal if there are resource constraints. Finally, older facilities actually have higher output for non-profits, while the effect for for-profits is essentially zero. Interestingly, Column 4 shows that concentration is weakly associated with higher-output per facility.

To check the robustness of the conclusion that for-profits have a static advantage in production, I considered the impact of a change in profit status on output for the subset of facilities whose status changed during the sample period. The evidence supports the idea that ownership structure is correlated with output. First, I considered the difference between the estimated $\bar{\hat{f}}$ for those facilities that switched to for-profit ownership and those that did not. This difference was statistically significant only when all values for the switchers were used but statistically insignificant when only the years prior to the change were used to identify the time invariant effects. Insofar as the effects identified with the entire sample period represent an average of the unobserved effects from before and after the profit-status transition, these results support the idea that for-profit status increases output. Furthermore, using models that control for time-invariant facility characteristics, time period, and county location, I find that those facilities that switched to for-profit status increased their output approximately 43 percent more than those that switched to non-profit status over a two year period.[32]

Overall, the results of analyses of hemodialysis production lend additional support to the hypothesis that for-profit facilities possess a static competitive advantage. I now turn to exploring whether entry patterns also support this perspective.

5.3 Rate of Entry

5.3.1 Empirical Approach

In order to understand the drivers of industry expansion across geographic markets, I estimate models of the general form:

$$E_{jmt} = E_j(X_{mt}, f_{jm} + e_{jmt}), \qquad (6)$$

where E_{jmt} is the total number of entrants of type j in market m at time t. In contrast to the

---

[32]Somewhat interestingly, there is evidence that becoming for-profit leads to lower output in the first year, perhaps indicating disruptive reorganization investments.

previous section, I allow each type of facility to have its own "birth" function of a set of market characteristics X_{mt}, a market fixed effect f_{jm}, and an i.i.d. error term e_{jmt}.

To estimate the different E_j, I exploit the conditional poisson model developed by Hausman et al. (1984). The traditional poisson model has a single parameter, λ, and would suggest that the probability of observing E_{jmt} entries of type j in market m at time t as:

$$\text{Prob}(E_{jmt}) = \frac{e^{-\lambda_j} \lambda_j^{E_{jmt}}}{E_{jmt}!}. \tag{7}$$

The conditional poisson model allows λ_j to vary both as a function of observable market characteristics X and unobserved, time-invariant fixed effect f:

$$\lambda_{jmt} = e^{X_{mt}\beta_j + f_{jm}}, \tag{8}$$

where β is the parameter vector of interest.

In order to understand how the conditional poisson approach addresses the possibility of consistent unobserved heterogeneity across markets, it is useful to review the likelihood function. Each element fed into the likelihood is the probability of observing the series of E_{jt} for each m:

$$\text{Prob}(E_{jm1}, ..., E_{jmT}) = \frac{e^{\sum_{t=1}^{T} \lambda_{jmt}} \prod_{t=1}^{T} \lambda_{jmt}^{E_{jmt}}}{(\prod_{t=1}^{T} E_{jmt})!}, \tag{9}$$

after conditioning out the total number of entrances of type j in market m over time:

$$\text{Prob}(\sum_{t=1}^{T} E_{jmt}) = \frac{e^{-\sum_{t=1}^{T} \lambda_{jmt}} (\sum_{t=1}^{T} \lambda_{jmt})^{\sum_{t=1}^{T} E_{jmt}}}{(\sum_{t=1}^{T} E_{jmt})!}. \tag{10}$$

By rearranging terms, the element in the likelihood function simplifies to:

$$\text{Prob}(E_{jm1}, ..., E_{jmT} | \sum_{t=1}^{T} E_{jmt}) = \prod_{t=1}^{T} \left(\frac{e^{X_{mt}\beta_j}}{\sum_{s=1}^{T} e^{X_{ms}\beta_j}} \right)^{E_{jmt}} \cdot \frac{(\sum_{t=1}^{T} E_{jmt})!}{\prod_{t=1}^{T} (E_{jmt}!)}. \tag{11}$$

Thus, the market-specific fixed effect cancels out of the likelihood function, facilitating computation and precluding the possibility of incidental parameters bias from estimating the market parameters directly in an unconditional model. Moreover, the estimates remain robust to time invariant differences across markets, perhaps the most important expected source of omitted variable bias. The model does have the implication, however, of not being able to identify parameters in markets that never experienced any entrances. Therefore, out of a total sample of 27653 county-year observations relating to 1763 counties, I am only able to use 15315 observations from 858 counties for the for-profit models and 6130 observations from 324 counties for the non-profit models.

For the entry models, I include a smaller set of covariates than in the models of exit and utilization. To proxy for demand, I use the lagged value of the log of the population over 60 (in 1000s). Similarly, I use lagged values of the various approaches to modeling the market structure. Since the models are more aggregated, I do not include facility-level detail on things like hospital affiliation or age. In essense, I am modeling the changes in market structure $\Delta\omega_{jt}$ as a function of the state of the world at $t - 1$.

In all models, I allow for the possibility of heteroskedastic standard errors. Calculating standard errors robust to violations of the assumption (implied by the poisson specification) that the conditional mean equals the conditional variance does not lead to dramatic changes in the statistical precision of the estimates (Wooldridge, 1999).

Table 7: Descriptive Statistics for Entry Samples

| | For-profit | | | Non-profit | | | |
	N	mean	sd	N	mean	sd	T-Stat
Entry	15315	0.21	0.61	6130	0.09	0.31	19.32
Log(Pop over 60)	15315	3.17	1.07	6130	3.61	1.16	-25.71
Log(Number of Competitors)	15315	1.23	0.67	6130	1.49	0.83	-22.33
Log(Number of For-profit)	15315	0.95	0.72	6130	0.99	0.93	-3.24
Log(Number of Non-profit)	15315	0.48	0.61	6130	0.89	0.66	-42.26
Log(Number of Unknown)	15315	0.01	0.11	6130	0.03	0.15	-6.75

5.3.2 Results

Table 7 shows summary statistics for the markets used in the analysis of for-profit and non-profit entry. Consistent with the descriptive evidence considered above, the Table shows much lower mean rates of entry for non-profit facilities. Interestingly, however, the Table indicates that despite on average being in smaller markets, new non-profit facilities have opened in larger markets than new for-profit facilities. This does not support the idea that non-profits systemattically target underserved, low demand areas.

Table 8 shows the results of three different pairs of models. Columns 1 and 2 show the coefficient results for models considering the impact of demand and market structure on the number of for-profit and non-profit facilities entering a given market without distinguishing between the competitive effects of for-profit and non-profit facilities. Columns 3 and 4 allow for different impacts depending on facility type. Columns 5 and 6 consider the possibility that the level of concentration could influence entry rates.

Because fixed effects cannot be identified in non-linear models such as the conditional poisson due to the incidental parameters problem (Wooldridge, 2002), I no longer provide mean estimated predicted effects. To gain insight, however, I re-estimated the models via linear panel methods – which lead to qualitatively similar results for the coefficients of interest finding that the average number of for-profit entrants is much larger when time-invariant heterogeneity is accounted for. These results can be found in Table B-4 in the Appendix.

Across all pairs of the conditional poisson models, I find that for-profit entry is more impacted by demand changes. Indeed, I find that for-profit entry is remarkably sensitive when the competitive environment is not disaggregated. The estimated coefficient in Column 1 implies an elasticity greater than 1. In other words, a 10 percent increase in the demand proxy would produce an almost 14 percent increase in entry. By contrast, the same increase in demand would only be expected to produce a 4 percent increase in the number of non-profits. Overall, these results support the idea that for-profit facilities have an advantage in static competition; however, they would also be consistent with the presence of lower entry costs.

The Table also provides additional evidence consistent with asymmetric competitive effects. Entry rates by for-profit and non-profit firms are both substantially more influenced by the presence of like facilities than they are unlike facilities. However, the data again show that the entry rate of non-profit facilities is quite impacted by the presence of for-profit competitors, while for-profits are not impacted at all by the presence of non-profit facilities. These results are consistent with the idea that for-profit dialysis facilities have a static advantage in attracting patients, treating patients at lower cost, or both.

Perhaps the most important takeaway from the entry results concerning market structure is that they are inconsistent with the idea that the rise of for-profit facilities stems entirely from having

Table 8: Entry as a Function of Demand & Competition

	(1) FP Entry b/se	(2) NP Entry b/se	(3) FP Entry b/se	(4) NP Entry b/se	(5) FP Entry b/se	(6) NP Entry b/se
Log(Pop over 60)	1.367***	0.433	0.425+	0.127	0.41	0.166
	0.35	0.74	0.32	0.74	0.32	0.73
Log(Number of Competitors)	-2.243***	-2.023***				
	0.16	0.29				
Log(Number of For-profit)			-1.336***	-0.789***	-1.352***	-0.757***
			0.17	0.16	0.18	0.17
Log(Number of Non-profit)			0.059	-1.151***	0.041	-1.071***
			0.12	0.21	0.13	0.24
Log(Number of Unknown)			0.004	-0.438	0.016	-0.482
			0.14	0.4	0.14	0.4
Log(HHI)					-0.037	0.127
					0.1	0.15
Year FE	Yes	Yes	Yes	Yes	Yes	Yes
County FE	Yes	Yes	Yes	Yes	Yes	Yes
N	15315	6130	15315	6130	15315	6130

* $p<0.10$, ** $p<0.05$, *** $p<0.01$ in 2-sided tests. + $p< 0.1$ in 1-sided tests. Standard errors are robust to heteroskedasticity.

lower average entry costs. If this were the case, then entry might be higher on average for them, but entry rates would not differ as a function of the local market structure. Thus, these results strongly suggest that variation in costs of capital do not explain much of the change in market structure over time in the dialysis industry relative to factors having to do with static competition.

While consistent with the patterns seen elsewhere, the overall precision of the estimates is markedly less than in models controling for greater facility level heterogeneity. Therefore, for robustness purposes, I ran several models examining the determinants of ownership status conditional on entry taking place. Consistent with the lack of precision in the market level results, I found considerable heterogeneity. Interestingly, I found that the two dominant chains were more responsive to changes in demand than non-profits, but that other for-profits were actually less so. These results suggest that, consistent with the rise of concentration, the large chains have some advantages not possessed by other competitors. Details on the simple conditional analyses described above are available upon request.

6 Conclusion

This paper has investigated the evolution of the dialysis industry over the last three decades, examining whether or not the evidence supports or contradicts different explanations for the rise of for-profit facilities. Consistent with much of the non-health care literature, I find evidence consistent with the longstanding hypothesis that for-profit organizations are more efficient (Alchian and Demsetz, 1972, Borjas et al., 1983, Philipson et al., 2010). This is also in line with the findings of several past papers on the dialysis industry in public health (Griffiths et al., 1994, Hirth et al., 1999, Ozgen and Ozcan, 2002). However, it runs contrary to a theoretical literature in health economics suggesting that a focus on output should lead non-profits to behave as though they had lower marginal costs (Lakdawalla and Philipson, 1998, 2006), which has found empirical support in studies focusing on hospitals (Sloan et al., 2001, Chakravarty et al., 2006).

In addition, I also find significant evidence consistent with the idea that diversion between facility types is quite asymmetric. In particular, diversion from for-profit to non-profit facilities appears less than from non-profit to for-profit. This could reflect higher perceived quality. Alternatively, it may stem from efforts to vertically integrate upstream with referring physicians by the major dialysis chains, which the largest chains are now emphasizing. In future work, I hope to focus more attention on this issue.

Overall, the policy implications of the analysis are ambiguous. For example, based on the revealed preference evidence documented in this paper, the replacement of all non-profit facilities by for-profit ones would occasion some utility loss (though whether of the referring doctors or the ultimate recipients of the treatments is not clear). That said, it would be unlikely to lead to substantial reduction in access to treatment. However, the overall implications for welfare analysis depend on factors not directly examined in this paper. In particular, they are highly dependent upon the existence and magnitude of the effects of competition and for-profit status on quality. I hope to investigate these issues in subsequent research. In addition, I hope to focus more attention on issues that arose in this paper; in particular, the likelihood of behavioral differences within the broader categories of for-profit and non-profit facilities, as well as the possible implications of DaVita and Fresenius' vertical expansions.

References

Alchian, Armen A. and Harold Demsetz, "Production, Information Costs, and Economic Organization," *The American Economic Review*, 1972, *62* (5), pp. 777–795.

Allison, Paul D. and Nicholas A. Christakis, "Fixed-Effects Methods for the Analysis of Nonrepeated Events," *Sociological Methodology*, 2006, *36*, 155–172.

Berry, S., "Estimation of a Model of Entry in the Airline Industry," *Econometrica*, 1992, *60*, 889–917.

Bloom, N. and J. Van Reenen, "Why do management practices differ across firms and countries?," *The Journal of Economic Perspectives*, 2010, *24* (1), 203–224.

Bloom, Nicholas, Raffaella Sadun, and John Van Reenen, "Americans Do IT Better: US Multinationals and the Productivity Miracle," *American Economic Review*, 2012, *102* (1), 167–201.

Borjas, George J., H. E. Frech III, and Paul B. Ginsburg, "Property Rights and Wages: The Case of Nursing Homes," *The Journal of Human Resources*, 1983, *18* (2), pp. 231–246.

Brooks, J.M., C.P. Irwin, L.G. Hunsicker, M.J. Flanigan, E.A. Chrischilles, and J.F. Pendergast, "Effect of Dialysis Center Profit-Status on Patient Survival: A Comparison of Risk-Adjustment and Instrumental Variable Approaches," *Health Services Research*, 2006, *41* (6), 2267–2289.

Chakravarty, S., M. Gaynor, S. Klepper, and W.B. Vogt, "Does the profit motive make Jack nimble? Ownership form and the evolution of the US hospital industry," *Health Economics*, 2006, *15* (4), 345–361.

Cutler, David, Leemore Dafny, and Christopher Ody, "Competition in Quality: The Case of U.S. Dialysis Clinics," *mimeo*, 2012.

DeOreo, P., "Reimbursement for Hemodialysis," *Hemodialysis Horizons*, 2006.

Dijk, C.E. Van, B. Berg, R.A. Verheij, P. Spreeuwenberg, P.P. Groenewegen, and D.H. Bakker, "Moral Hazard and Supplier-Induced Demand: Empirical Evidence in General Practice," *Health Economics*, 2012.

Doraszelski, U. and M. Satterthwaite, "Computable Markov-Perfect Industry Dynamics," *The RAND Journal of Economics*, 2007, *41* (2), 215–243.

Ericson, R. and A. Pakes, "Markov-perfect industry dynamics: A framework for empirical work," *The Review of Economic Studies*, 1995, *62* (1), 53–82.

Farley, D.O., "Effects of Competition of Dialysis Facility Service Levels and Patient Selection," RAND Corporation Ph.D. Dissertation 1993.

Ford, J.M. and D.L. Kaserman, "Certificate-of-need regulation and entry: Evidence from the dialysis industry," *Southern Economic Journal*, 1993, pp. 783–791.

_ and _ , "Ownership structure and the quality of medical care: evidence from the dialysis industry," *Journal of Economic Behavior & Organization*, 2000, *43* (3), 279–293.

Garg, P.P., K.D. Frick, M. Diener-West, and N.R. Powe, "Effect of the ownership of dialysis facilities on patients' survival and referral for transplantation," *New England Journal of Medicine*, 1999, *341* (22), 1653–1660.

Gaynor, M. and R.J. Town, "Competition in health care markets," Technical Report, National Bureau of Economic Research 2011.

Gaynor, Martin, Samuel A. Kleiner, and William B. Vogt, "A Structural Approach to Market Definition With an Application to the Hospital Industry," Working Paper 16656, National Bureau of Economic Research January 2011.

Grieco, P.L.E. and R.C. McDevitt, "Productivity and Quality in Health Care: Evidence from the Dialysis Industry," *mimeo*, 2012.

Griffiths, R.I., N.R. Powe, D.J. Gaskin, G.F. Anderson, G.V. de Lissovoy, and P.K. Whelton, "The production of dialysis by for-profit versus not-for-profit freestanding renal dialysis facilities.," *Health Services Research*, 1994, *29* (4), 473.

Harrison, T.D. and C.A. Laincz, "Entry and Exit in the Nonprofit Sector," *The BE Journal of Economic Analysis & Policy*, 2008, *8* (1).

Hausman, Jerry, Bronwyn H. Hall, and Zvi Griliches, "Econometric Models for Count Data with an Application to the Patents-R & D Relationship," *Econometrica*, 1984, *52* (4), pp. 909–938.

Held, P.J. and M.V. Pauly, "Competition and efficiency in the end stage renal disease program," *Journal of Health Economics*, 1983, *2* (2), 95–118.

Helmchen, L.A. and A.T. Lo Sasso, "How sensitive is physician performance to alternative compensation schedules? Evidence from a large network of primary care clinics," *Health Economics*, 2010, *19* (11), 1300–1317.

Hennig-Schmidt, Heike, Reinhard Selten, and Daniel Wiesen, "How payment systems affect physicians provision behaviourAn experimental investigation," *Journal of Health Economics*, 2011, *30* (4), 637 – 646.

Hirth, R.A., PJ Held, SM Orzol, and A. Dor, "Practice patterns, case mix, Medicare payment policy, and dialysis facility costs.," *Health Services Research*, 1999, *33* (6), 1567.

Lakdawalla, D. and T. Philipson, "The nonprofit sector and industry performance," *Journal of Public Economics*, 2006, *90* (8), 1681–1698.

Lakdawalla, Darius and Tomas Philipson, "Nonprofit Production and Competition," Working Paper 6377, National Bureau of Economic Research January 1998.

Lee, D.K.K., G.M. Chertow, and S.A. Zenios, "Reexploring Differences among For-Profit and Nonprofit Dialysis Providers," *Health Services Research*, 2010, *45* (3), 633–646.

Mazzeo, M.J., "Product choice and oligopoly market structure," *RAND Journal of Economics*, 2002, pp. 221–242.

Ozgen, H. and Y. A. Ozcan, "A national study of efficiency for dialysis centers: an examination of market competition and facility characteristics for production of multiple dialysis outputs," *Health Services Research*, 2002, *37* (3), 711–732.

Pakes, A. and P. McGuire, "Computing Markov-Perfect Nash Equilibria: Numerical Implications of a Dynamic Differentiated Product Model," *RAND Journal of Economics*, 1994, *25* (4), 555–589.

_ , **M. Ostrovsky, and S. Berry**, "Simple estimators for the parameters of discrete dynamic games (with entry/exit examples)," *The RAND Journal of Economics*, 2007, *38* (2).

Philipson, T. J., S. A. Seabury, L. M. Lockwood, D. P. Goldman, D. N. Lakdawalla, and D. M. Cutler, "Geographic Variation in Health Care: The Role of Private Markets [with Comment and Discussion]," *Brookings Papers on Economic Activity*, 2010, pp. 325–361.

Pozniak, A.S., R.A. Hirth, J. Banaszak-Holl, and J.R.C. Wheeler, "Predictors of Chain Acquisition among Independent Dialysis Facilities," *Health Services Research*, 2010, *45* (2), 476–496.

Ramanarayanan, S. and J. Snyder, "Reputation and Firm Performance: Evidence from the Dialysis Industry," *mimeo*, 2012.

Schlesinger, M. and B.H. Gray, "How nonprofits matter in American medicine, and what to do about it," *Health Affairs*, 2006, *25* (4), W287–W303.

Sloan, F.A., G.A. Picone, D.H. Taylor Jr, and S.Y. Chou, "Hospital ownership and cost and quality of care: is there a dime's worth of difference?," *Journal of Health Economics*, 2001, *20* (1), 1–21.

_ , **T.J. Hoerger, M.A. Morrisey, and M. Hassan**, "The demise of hospital philanthropy," *Economic Inquiry*, 1990, *28* (4), 725–743.

Swanson, A., "Physician Ownership and Incentives: Evidence from Cardiac Care," *University of Pennsylvania*, mimeo, 2012.

USRDS, "United States Renal Data System Annual Report," Technical Report, United States Renal Data System 2011.

Wilson, N.E., "Uncertain regulatory timing and market dynamics," *International Journal of Industrial Organization*, 2012, *30* (1), 120–115.

Wooldridge, J. M., *Econometric analysis of cross section and panel data*, The MIT press, 2002.

Wooldridge, J.M., "Distribution-free estimation of some nonlinear panel data models," *Journal of Econometrics*, 1999, *90* (1), 77–97.

Zhang, Y., D.J. Cotter, and M. Thamer, "The effect of dialysis chains on mortality among patients receiving hemodialysis," *Health Services Research*, 2011, *46* (3), 747–767.

A   Theoretical Model Details

Below, I quickly describe the details of the theoretical model used to generate the Figures from Section 4 of the text. As noted above, the model is in the Ericson and Pakes (1995) class of models, bearing the closest resemblance to that used in Pakes et al. (2007). I assume that demand is in long-run equilibrium and then experiences unexpected shocks that market participants do not anticipate. Incorporating rational (or otherwise) expectations about the possibility of the shocks as is done in Pakes et al. (2007) or Wilson (2012) would be a simple, yet tedious, process, requiring that the different possibilities include an additional loop characterizing the different demand states. I do not believe there is sufficient probative value in the current setting from formally accounting for this factor to justify the additional computational complexity.

A.1   Static Competition

As noted above, I model demand in a simple way designed to capture the most salient characteristics of the retail dialsysis industry. In particular, I fix the price p that all market participants receive per dialyzation performed. The share of total demand, Q_{mt}, served by a particular facility i of type f is determined according to a modification of the familiar Hotelling model of differentiated demand.

If demand is not horizontally differentiated, then I impose that it is equally shared amongst all market participants. If, however, demand is purely horizontally differentiated by factor γ, where $\gamma \in [0, 0.5]$, then I assign facilities' locations on the Hotelling line in the following way. Assume that there are n_l low-cost and n_h high-cost facilities, and that $n_l + n_h = N$ total facilities. Then, when $n_l \geq n_h$, define the "boundary" point h on the Hotelling line as $h = \frac{n_l}{N} - (n_l - n_h) * \gamma$. I assume then that all n_l are distributed such that they each serve $\frac{h}{n_l}$ of the total market, while each high-cost facility serves exactly $\frac{1-h}{n_h}$. (Should $n_h > n_l$, an analogous approach determines the boundary point and individual facilities' shares.)

Although somewhat idiosyncratic, this approach straightforwardly accommodates horizontal demand differentiation, assuming that roughly equal shares of the population prefer each type of facility. As γ approaches 0.5, consumers so strongly prefer one type of facility that entrants only cannibalize the treatments performed by others of the same type. Alternatively, as γ converges on 0, consumers do not prefer one type of facility to another, and all facilities in the market will perform an equal number of treatments.

A.2 Dynamic Factors

I largely follow the approach taken in Pakes et al. (2007) with respect to the stochastic entry and exit distributions. Thus, I assume that all ξ and κ represent draws from exponential distributions. The choice of the exponential distribution is unapologetically made to simplify computation. As noted in Pakes et al. (2007), it implies that the expected payoff of choosing to exit conditional on a given market structure configuration can be written as:

$$E(\xi|\xi > VC(Q,\omega)) = VC(Q,\omega) + \sigma, \tag{12}$$

assuming that ξ is distributed exponentially with cdf $F(\xi) = 1 - \exp(-\frac{1}{\sigma}\xi)$. Similarly, the probability of entering can be computed in the following manner. First, establish whether the value of entry exceeds the minimum entry cost, κ:

$$M \;=\; \max(0, \beta * VE(Q,\omega) - \kappa 0). \tag{13}$$

Then, the probability that entry occurs is simply:

$$\Pr(entry) \;=\; 1 - \exp(-\alpha * M) * (1 + \alpha * M), \tag{14}$$

where κ is exponentially distributed with parameter α.

A.3 Parameterization

In developing the Figures used in the paper to illustrate the implications of variation in economic primitives for market structure evolution, I explored a variety of parameterizations to ensure the robustness of the results. For the specific results presented in the text, however, I parameterized the model as follows.

In all models I assume that the fixed price $p = 1.5$, the discount factor β is 0.9, the exit draw parameter σ is 0.5, and that the maximum number of each type of facility is 8. I also assume that static competition entails paying a fixed cost of 1 per period.

For the level of demand when marginal costs differ, I assume that $Q = 10$ or $Q = 12$. My assumption is that high-cost facilities' marginal costs are 10 percent higher than those for low-cost facilities, which is set to 1. Thus, for Figure 5 (Figure 6), I contrast the calculated exit (entry) policy functions when $Q = 10$ relative to when $Q = 12$ holding all else constant. Figure 7 is produced using $Q = 12$.

When examining the implications of entry cost variation, I increase low-cost facilities' marginal costs to the same level as high-cost facilities. When focusing on the impact of variation in marginal costs, I assume that both types of facilities have entry cost parameters α of 0.5 and that their minimum cost of entry is $\frac{1}{\alpha} = 2$. When focusing on the impact of variation in entry cost, I keep both α's the same, but set the minimum cost of entry for the low-cost type at 1.6 instead of 2. Demand is set at $Q = 12$ for Figure 8 in order to ensure comparability with Figure 7.

I present no results for the impact of allowing for horizontal differentiation, keeping γ fixed at 0 in all models. However, in unincluded results, I experimented with a number of alternative parameterizations. The results were intuitive.

A.4 Computation

All programs were written and run in Matlab 7.4. I solve for facilities' equilibrium strategies using a variant of the Gaussian procedure described in Pakes and McGuire (1994). The limiting distribution was found by first calculating a large matrix indicating the likelihood of transitioning from one state to another from one time period to the next. This matrix was raised to higher and higher power until it converged on the limiting distribution.

Code for all aspects of the modeling is available upon request.

B Additional Tables

Table B-1: Chain Identities and For-Profit Status

Chain Name	First Year	Last Year	Total Obs	For-Profit Obs	Non-Profit Obs
ARA	2005	2008	237	237	0
DAVITA	1995	2008	8886	8886	0
DCI	1988	2008	2846	0	2846
EVEREST	1996	2008	171	171	0
FRESENIUS	1988	2008	15651	15651	0
GAMBRO	1996	2008	4902	4902	0
INDT	1988	2008	35441	16806	18193
LIBERTY	2008	2008	41	41	0
NATIONAL	1999	2008	388	388	0
NRA	2006	2008	101	101	0
NRI	2006	2008	243	243	0
RCG	1996	2008	2876	2876	0
REGDCA	2005	2008	123	123	0
REGRRI	2005	2008	144	144	0
REGSATHC	2006	2008	108	108	0
RENALADVAN	2005	2008	296	296	0
RTC	1993	1997	357	357	0
VIVRA	1988	2008	1298	1298	0

Table B-2: Conditional Logit Estimates of the Likelihood of Exit

	(1) b/se	(2) b/se	(3) b/se
1(For-profit)	2.93	-3.57	3.221
	3.68	4.71	11.92
Log(Pop over 60)	-2.970**	-4.541***	-5.550***
	1.33	1.66	1.69
Log(Pop over 60) * For-Profit	1.850+	3.658**	4.275***
	1.16	1.5	1.57
Hospital Affiliated	1.943	2.01	1.9
	2.03	1.96	1.96
Hospital Affiliated * For-profit	-2.351	-1.513	-1.221
	1.89	1.76	1.77
Time since certification	1.393***	1.367***	1.352***
	0.09	0.08	0.08
Time since certification * For-profit	0.507***	0.576***	0.573***
	0.11	0.09	0.1
Log(Number of Competitors)	10.197***		
	0.96		
Log(Number of Competitors) * For-profit	-5.057***		
	1.19		
Log(Number of For-profit)		12.101***	13.765***
		1.09	1.27
Log(Number of For-profit) * For-profit		-5.410***	-5.846***
		1.33	1.44
Log(Number of Non-profit)		2.679***	4.709***
		0.74	1.12
Log(Number of Non-profit) * For-profit		-2.824***	-3.972***
		0.96	1.35
Log(Number of Unknown)		5.047***	5.870***
		1.76	1.77
Log(Number of Unknown) * For-profit		-4.856**	-5.255***
		1.91	1.94
Log(HHI)			3.012**
			1.24
Log(HHI) * For-profit			-0.979
			1.32
Status * Year FE	No	No	No
Facility FE	Yes	Yes	Yes
Chain FE	No	No	No
N	8641	8641	8641

* $p<0.10$, ** $p<0.05$, *** $p<0.01$ in 2-sided tests. + $p< 0.1$ in 1-sided test.

Table B-3: Additional Models of Hemodialysis Treatment Production

	(1) b/se	(2) b/se	(3) b/se	(4) b/se
1(For-profit)	-0.036	0.178*	-0.138***	-0.081
	0.03	0.1	0.03	0.21
Log(Pop over 60)	0.895***	0.863***	0.813***	0.775***
	0.07	0.07	0.07	0.06
Hospital Affiliated	0.042***	0.042***	0.010**	0.009*
	0	0	0	0
Time since certification	-0.820***	-0.793***	-0.442***	-0.388***
	0.05	0.05	0.07	0.07
Log(Number of Competitors)	-0.737***	-0.732***	-0.540***	-0.531***
	0.02	0.02	0.02	0.02
County FE	Yes	Yes	No	No
Year	Yes	Yes	Yes	Yes
Facility FE	No	No	Yes	Yes
Chain FE	No	Yes	No	Yes
N	65373	65373	65373	65373

* p<0.10, ** p<0.05, *** p<0.01 in 2-sided tests. + p< 0.1 in 1-sided test. Standard errors clustered at facility level.

Table B-4: Linear Entry Models

	(1) FP Entry b/se	(2) NP Entry b/se	(3) FP Entry b/se	(4) NP Entry b/se	(5) FP Entry b/se	(6) NP Entry b/se
Log(Pop over 60)	0.192***	0.122*	0.120*	0.091+	0.135**	0.091+
	0.07	0.07	0.07	0.07	0.07	0.07
Log(Number of Competitors)	-0.273***	-0.187***				
	0.02	0.02				
Log(Number of For-profit)			-0.195***	-0.096***	-0.145***	-0.099***
			0.02	0.02	0.03	0.02
Log(Number of Non-profit)			0.021	-0.117***	0.083**	-0.124***
			0.03	0.02	0.04	0.02
Log(Number of Unknown)			0.104	-0.055+	0.068	-0.052+
			0.1	0.04	0.1	0.04
Log(HHI)					0.098***	-0.01
					0.04	0.02
Predicted Non-Profit	0.10		0.10		0.10	
Predicted For-Profit	0.37		0.37		0.37	
P-value of H0: diff == 0	0.00		0.00		0.00	
Year FE	Yes	Yes	Yes	Yes	Yes	Yes
County FE	Yes	Yes	Yes	Yes	Yes	Yes
N	15315	6130	15315	6130	15315	6130

* p<0.10, ** p<0.05, *** p<0.01 in 2-sided tests. + p< 0.1 in 1-sided tests. Standard errors clustered at the county level.